Have you seen Baby Hippo?
It's time for him to come home.

He must be here somewhere!

Is he hiding in Hummingbird's honeysuckle?

Is he hiding in Hedgehog's hole?

Is he hiding in Hare's hutch?

Is he hiding in the hens' house?

Is he hiding in Horse's haystack?

Is he hiding behind the honeybees' hive?

Is he hiding in the hyenas' hideaway?

Where could Baby Hippo be hiding?
Mother Hippo has something for him...

...a great big hippo hug!

How many things can you find that begin with the letter H?

See inside back cover for answers.

Hh Cheer

H is for honeybee, H is for hen

H is for hamster and hogs in a pen

H is for hiccups, hat, hug, and horse

H is for hula-hoop and hippo of course

Hooray for H, big and small—

the happiest, hoppiest letter of all!